Beyond Passion

Henry Fernandez

Beyond Passion

Henry Fernandez

Evergreen PRESS

Beyond Passion
by Henry Fernandez

©2001 Henry Fernandez

All rights reserved. This book is protected under the copyright laws of the United States of America. This book may not be copied or reprinted for commercial gain or profit. The use of short quotations is permitted and encouraged. Unless otherwise identified, Scripture quotations are taken from the King James Version of the Bible.

ISBN 1-58169-068-1
For worldwide distribution.
Printed in the U.S.A.

Evergreen Press
P.O. Box 91011 • Mobile, AL 36691
800-367-8203

Table of Contents

1. The Secret of Finding What God Has for You 1
2. Beginning to Date 13
3. Marriage, an Honorable State 19
4. Overcoming the Flesh 27
5. Keeping Your Body Holy 37
6. Temptations of the Flesh 47
7. Dealing With Temptation 59
8. Pressures Singles Have to Deal With 71
9. Loneliness and Isolation 81
10. Sexual Pressure 87
11. Parenting 93
12. Insufficiency 101
13. Under Construction 105

Dedication

To all the singles at The Faith Center who untiringly support the vision and mission of the ministry, I dedicate this book to you. Remember, no one can make you feel insufficient or inferior because of your status in a relationship, unless you consent to other people's opinion and belief. You may be waiting to get married or you're separated, widowed, or divorced at this time, but having the knowledge of biblical truths for dating will definitely be of interest if you choose to change your relationship status in the future. Christ is able to keep you through any situation and guide you through all temptation. Keep on serving Christ by living to please Him and Him alone!

Dedication

To Clavel (Sharon) and Condeta (Joan) my two older sisters: I encourage you both to continue serving Christ to the best of your ability. Keep on aspiring to reach your goals, not just on a spiritual level, but on a relational, social, financial, and emotional level. Give your desires to God and remember He's the only one that can direct your paths. I pray that as you continue to grow in God, He'll answer your every need. Be persistent, assertive, and challenge every obstacle that is placed in your path. You are destined to be winners!

Introduction

It's easy to see that secular society "ministers" to our Christian singles. The television feeds their minds with programs that work on their emotions and tells them how to love. Movies, magazines, and the tabloids depict the worldly view of dating. The world's viewpoint can become the norm for our singles because they hear more of it than the Christian viewpoint.

We Christians tend to ignore singles as if they don't need any special help. For some reason the church shies away from the issue of singleness. We know some of the things the singles in our church go through, but we somehow tend to sweep these issues under the table. Many churches focus on evangelism, instead. We focus on reaching the world and trying to get people saved. But as we get people saved through the preaching of the Word, we need to make sure that we have a program that will help the singles in their everyday lives so they can remain in the kingdom. Because if we don't, just as sure as they walk in the front door, they're going to walk out the back.

Sometimes singles have a hard time relating to those of us who are married because we don't have to deal with some of the issues that they do. They confront hundreds of temptations on a constant basis—daily, weekly, and monthly. The enemy tries to destroy them so he does everything he can to prevent them from ever getting married. He knows that God honors a couple who take their wedding vows. When a couple does not elevate their relationship into a covenant marriage, the church needs to help them or we are going to lose them.

One of the ways we can help our singles is with developing powerful singles' ministries in our churches and counseling departments where they can receive guidance for some of the challenges in their lives. We need to be creative in order to meet their special needs.

There are many Christian singles out there who want to live pure and holy lives. They'll tell you that they're faced with tough decisions. They need to know how to move a relationship from the let's-just-go-out-and-meet-each-other stage into serious dating. All of these concerns are very important to single people. They know what they want. They want someone they can settle down with, someone they can start a family with. Most singles are looking for someone with whom they can walk together and fulfill God's plan for their lives. Unfortunately, very few messages are addressed to them. They're left alone to find things out, and sometimes they resort to secular books and television programs that will, in all probability, lead them astray.

These are the people to whom I write this book. I want you to enjoy the dating experience and find the person God has especially chosen for you. May your lives be richly blessed!

God has given us practical guidance to help men and women learn how to become united in a successful, fulfilling marriage today. God has not changed over the centuries and neither have His people—we still have the same needs, desires, and temptations.

CHAPTER ONE

The Secret of Finding What God Has for You

Who can find a virtuous woman? for her price is far above rubies.

The heart of her husband doth safely trust in her, so that he shall have no need of spoil.

She will do him good and not evil all the days of her life. (Proverbs 31:10-12)

Dating in the 21st century may seem like centuries away from the verses above. However, through these and other scriptures, God has given us practical guidance to help men and women learn how to become united in a successful, fulfilling marriage today. God has not changed over the centuries and neither have His people—we still have the same needs, desires, and temptations. The plan He spells out in His Word is one that will take people of the 21st century through the sometimes difficult path of dating to the satisfying state of matrimony.

Looking for a Wife

God's plan for finding a mate begins with a man looking for a wife as stated in the verse above, "Who can find a virtuous woman?" And Proverbs 18:22 says, "He who finds a wife finds a good thing." Both of these scriptures give us a clear indication that it should be the man who finds the woman, and not the woman who finds the man.

Contrary to this scripture, men in the church have been taught in the past that they committed sin just by looking at a woman. In order to keep us out of trouble, people who meant well did an injustice to us by misquoting the following scripture: "But I say unto you, that whosoever looketh on a woman to lust after her hath committed adultery with her already in his heart" (Matt. 5:28). These well-meaning people taught us: "When you look at a woman, you lust." That is *not* what the Bible says. Looking does not necessarily get you in trouble. It's the thoughts you entertain in your mind *after* you look that can present a problem.

Those of you who feel guilty just because you have looked at a woman sometimes play a little game of hide and seek. If you see a woman you like, you think you must hide the fact and don't pursue her as you'd like to. Thus God's plan is not followed. Many times this forces the woman to pursue the man, which is not biblical. You need not be timid about pursuing a woman—the Bible gives single men every right to search for and find a virtuous woman. You should also be aware that not every woman is virtuous, so you should *actively search* in order to find one. But when you do, you need to keep your mind, heart, and thoughts clear to prevent future disaster.

Sometimes the opposite problem occurs in today's world. Men look at women without thinking twice about it. They look at women wherever and whenever they feel like it. But it's necessary to remember that there's a time and a place for everything. For instance, during a worship service is *not* the proper time to look for a woman. (Unfortunately, there are some men who attend church *only* when they're looking for a wife because they know virtuous women attend church.) So don't come to church, look around in the middle of praise and worship, and begin to sing, "Thank you, God, I praise you" because you see someone who you think might be right for you. There are many other times when it is proper to look for a wife.

The secret of finding the one who is meant to be yours is to understand your position as a man. God wants *you*, the man, to take the initiative in finding your woman. You have to be careful, some women who pursue men are not virtuous.

Waiting for a Man

All the women who feel desperate about getting married need to stop looking and let the men find them. This is scriptural. Don't go after him; don't listen to the system of the world. The world says to women without husbands that the first man who comes around is their last chance, so they should grab him. Don't listen to the world. You need to realize in your heart how precious you are. You also need to wait for the man God has purposed to be your husband.

When a woman is found by her man, she should

not respond too quickly to him. It's good for a woman to let him *work for her*. In other words, he must do things to win her love and trust. Remember how Jacob worked 14 long years for Rachel? Of course that's not what happens today, but nevertheless, it doesn't hurt him to "sweat" for you. When he ends up winning you, he'll understand that you're priceless.

While waiting for your man to find you, there are times when your feelings of loneliness will be great. You can be in a room filled with thousands of people and feel all alone as though no one cares. You ache to find the one person you can spend the rest of your life with. God understands your feelings. He knows that you need a husband just as much as a man needs a wife. It's His desire to give you that husband. He wants you to be in love with a man and walk together in unity. Our God is an affectionate God. He will never leave you nor forsake you (Heb. 13:5). When these feelings come, God can wrap His arms around you right in the midst of it and let you know that He loves you.

God knows that a woman needs a man's love and affection. He wants to give you a husband who will hug you and give you that affection. But if you don't want to hear about love, perhaps it's because you have emotional scars from a bad relationship. Perhaps someone has left you in the past, and now you have no desire to be with anyone. You need to begin to ask God to help you prepare for your next relationship. Don't let your past experience hinder what God has for you to receive in the future. So what if someone left you? Maybe the Lord, in His mercy, caused the breakup Himself. Remember, all things work together for your good (Rom. 8:28).

Families Are Part of God's Plan

In the Garden of Eden, God created Adam and Eve and told them to be fruitful and multiply. He created them for each other and for the children who would be the fruit of their marriage. Families are all important to God's plan for mankind. Sometimes we get so "spiritual" that we neglect them. We come to church and hug our brothers and sisters next to us, but forget that our wife or husband or children also need to be hugged. God is not pleased with that kind of neglect. A man especially needs to remember that God wants to join him to a wife, and she needs a man to give her hugs and to love and appreciate her. Show her some affection. She is priceless. So when you're married, you need to show her how much you love her.

The Secret of Finding What God Has for You

Understanding Value

A man needs to *find* a woman, but a woman need to *know her own value*. A woman cannot just let a man come into her life and get "freebies." The gospel is not free—Jesus paid a price for our sins. Neither are you free; woman, you are priceless. When a man finds you, remember that. He cannot buy you a dozen roses and expect to take you to bed. He has to understand that a dozen roses cannot buy you. You can buy *yourself* two dozen roses any time. You need to remember that you cannot be bought with flowers or any material things because you are priceless.

> *A capable, intelligent and virtuous woman, who can find her. She is far more precious than jewelry and her value is far above rubies or pearls.*
>
> *The heart of her husband trusts in her comfortably and relies confidently, and believes in her securely, so that he has no lack of honest gain or need of dishonest spoil* (Prov. 31:10-11 Amp.).

Verse 11 implies that a woman makes the man. Men, do you see why it's important that you find a woman who has value? Whatever woman you take, she is going to help create you. If you take someone without any values, you'll lose yours too. The Bible says a woman is the *heart* of her husband. He should be able to trust in her confidently, rely on her, and believe in her. Women, you have to put yourself in a position where a husband can believe in you, trust you, and know your worth. He has to be able to say about you, "I know my woman. She would never do anything dishonest."

The Bible encourages each of you to add to the other. The woman's character is going to help shape you into the man you're going to be. It's so important when you're searching for a woman that you search for one who is priceless. Likewise, women, it's very important that the man who finds you is a man who recognizes your true worth.

Women, you don't realize what you're doing when you get together with your girlfriends and complain about your fiancé and call him a "dog." What does that say *about you* when you berate him to others and yet are committed to a relationship with him? What does that do to your *value?*

Your man should be able to trust in you and know that you aren't going to gossip about him with your girlfriends and share his secrets with them. Your future husband should be able to leave the house knowing that you won't do anything to destroy the kingdom that he's trying to build.

The same thing goes for single men who are dating. They should not tell their fiancée's secrets to the world. She should be able to trust him. If he can't uphold her confidence, he needs to rethink the relationship.

Comfort and Encouragement

In the Amplified Bible, Proverbs 31:12 describes another important aspect of a priceless woman. It says, "She comforts and encourages." It does *not* say she nags and nags. Men, do you see how important it is that you go after a woman who is priceless? You have to consider how she'll treat you. Don't go after someone who only *looks* beautiful. Beauty changes. The best way to find a woman is to observe her for awhile. Forget her outward appearance. There are women who look nice on the outside with immaculate nails and hair. They may be pretty on the outside, but they might have a nasty attitude or they might be full of themselves. Be careful not to get attracted just by what you see. You have to love the person who's on the inside.

Beyond Passion

The comfort that God talks about in Proverbs 31 is for a woman to make a man feel wanted, to make him feel like a man. A woman needs to build up a man's ego. Any time you kill a man's ego, you kill the strength of the man. Tell him, "You got it going on, baby"—even if he doesn't. You're projecting what you know that *he can become.* "I love you. You are my man." When you do this, you'll comfort and encourage him.

On the other hand, when you nag—whether you're in a relationship or a marriage (and this goes for a man or a woman)—you're driving the other person away from you by words such as, "You were *supposed* to empty the garbage, but it's still piling up in the kitchen. When are you going to take it out?" No one wants to hear something with that attitude. Use a little psychology. Let's say your man is not doing what you would like him to do. Call him in and say, "Honey, I know I asked you to empty the garbage, but it's not emptied yet. You know, baby, I know you can do it." It sounds funny, but it's a much better approach. "Please take the garbage out for me. Pookie, can you just do that for me?" When you say it this way, your man can't find the garbage bin fast enough. *Where's the garbage? Let me get it. She called me Pookie!* Now he willingly accomplishes his least favorite task for the first time with a smile on his face and a bounce in his step. Any time a woman knows how to talk to her man the right way, she will be blessed.

Likewise, women, don't respond only to someone who *looks* handsome and has lots of muscles. That changes with time. Muscles can soon become soft. If you just look at the outward appearance, you could make the biggest mistake of your life. You should love the other person because of what is within them.

As men and women seek God about who they should date, following His plan will protect them and bring them happiness.

When a woman and man start to kiss and show affection, it's dangerous. God has built something in man called body chemistry. When a woman touches you and you begin to kiss, it's going to take more than what you learned in church last week to stop you from going any further!

Chapter Two

Beginning to Date

How do you approach a young lady to ask her out? The first thing you might do is go over to her and say, "You know, I've been noticing you (at church, etc). I don't know if you'd mind, but I'd love to take you out on a dinner date. Is that okay?" Be mellow.

Women, what you can do now is let him sweat. You may say in your heart, *Thank you, Jesus, you have answered my prayers, God!* But what should come out of your mouth is, "That's nice, but I'm sorry. I can't give you an answer right now. Can you give me some time to think about it?" Even though you really want to go, don't give him a quick answer. If he's really interested in you, no matter what you ask him to do, he's going to be persistent.

Men, don't force yourself on the woman. Go back again a second time, if she put you off. Ask her again by saying, "Look, I know it's been two weeks, and I'm not asking you for anything big, just a dinner date." The woman can ask where he intends to take her. If he says, "I was just thinking about having a nice private dinner at my place"—look out! The Bible instructs us to shun the very appearance of evil (1 Thes. 5:22). Your reply to him should be: "I have a policy of not visiting with men alone in their homes." Watch his response. If he looks down on you for your answer, it's time to take a big step backwards in the relationship.

On the first date, men, take her to a restaurant. Don't take her just anywhere, use wisdom. Take her out to a nice restaurant and then drive her home and thank her for the great time you had together. If you think you may want to see her again, it would be good to wait awhile before you call her.

Women, if a man approaches you one Sunday after church and says, "I've been watching you for a couple of weeks, and the Lord told me that you're going to be my wife"—you might recommend that he talk to the pastor and get some counseling. Any man that speaks to you like that in the first conversation will probably not make a good husband. He's actually saying, "God spoke to me, and you have no say in it whatsoever." Men, that's not the proper way to address a young lady in order to ask her out. And don't tell her a bunch of tired, she-has-heard-it-all-before stuff such as: "You look so beautiful. I've been watching you, and you sweep me off my feet." All of that is cheap talk. Any woman who falls for those lines has devalued her worth.

Check Him Out

Before you have a second date, woman, you should ask around about him. Call your friends and see if they know anything about him. Talk to his pastor and ask about him and his family and whether or not he can recommend his character. Don't try to to stir up gossip about him, but do be careful for your own safety.

You should be aware of any potential problems from a man's past so that if something comes to light you won't be alarmed. It's better for you to be careful than to develop a serious relationship with someone who professes to be a sheep but is really a wolf in disguise.

Stay Away From Temptation

When you're dating, it's best to avoid situations where you might be tempted to let the flesh take over. You're both still human. You're saved but not yet delivered from the flesh. When you entertain one another, avoid being alone. If you go to her house or she comes to your house, make sure there are other people present. If you meet at a private place where it's just the two of you, you're creating a situation that you might not be able to handle. As much as you love the Lord, you may find yourselves doing things that you shouldn't be doing. One of you may say, "Well, you know, we've been going out for about three months. Now that we're alone, can I get a kiss?" And of course the devil says to you, "What's a little kiss?"

Men, you have to understand you're built differently than a woman. Most women can probably kiss you and still maintain control. Men, you know your weakness. You won't find anywhere in the Bible where it says, "Don't put your tongue in somebody's mouth," but the Bible *does* say to shun the very appearance of evil. Walk away from trouble before it begins. When a woman and man start to kiss and show affection, it's dangerous. God has built something in man called body chemistry. When a woman touches you and you begin to kiss, it's going to take more than what you learned in church last week to stop you from going any further!

Many single Christians have been caught in a trap. You didn't want to, but you did. How did it happen? It began with just holding hands. Of course there's nothing wrong with that. Then it progressed from holding hands to a hug. There's nothing wrong with that either as long as you don't get too close. Then you kissed and the situation rapidly progressed to petting. Before you knew it, the sin was committed. You walked away and said, "I really didn't want to do it, God." Let's not sugarcoat this topic. God wants you to be together, but he wants you to do it *His way*.

God's plan is one that will bring blessing upon the man and woman when they enter the marriage covenant. Before they do that, however, there are some things about the very foundation of your relationship that you'll need to understand.

God has given you the privilege of dating in order that your dating will lead to the honorable position of marriage. Dating only takes you from one stage to the next. It was never God's intention for you to continue to date someone forever.

CHAPTER THREE

Marriage, an Honorable State

Marriage is honourable in all, and the bed undefiled: but whoremongers and adulterers God will judge. (Hebrews 13:4)

The verse above states that marriage is an honorable state. It's important to emphasize this truth. When a man and woman are drawn together in love, the next step is to be an honorable one. Dating should lead towards the honorable environment, which is marriage. You aren't worthy of experiencing all that the union between two people has to offer until you're in a marriage covenant. When you're single, God has given you the *privilege* of dating in order that your dating will lead to the honorable position of marriage. Dating only takes you from one stage to the next. It was never God's intention for you to continue to date someone forever. If you meet a person, begin dating them, declare your love, but have no intention of ever getting married to them, you're being unfair. If you say, "I don't want to get married. Can we just be friends?", you're toying with their emotions. Worldly people do things like that without any pang of conscience because they have no intention of meeting anyone else's needs, only their own. God's plan, on the other hand, is one of mutual care and concern and happiness for you both.

Two Categories of Singles

All singles fall into one of two categories. Category one is the single person desiring to marry. To the question, "Do you really have a desire to get married?", most singles quickly answer "Yes!" But there are some singles who say, "I don't want to get married. Me and Jesus got something going on." Don't kid yourself. You're not fooling anybody. You say that publicly, but when you're home alone, you can't cover it up anymore—you're sometimes lonely and depressed. You look up at the ceiling and say, "Jesus, please send me a partner. Help me find someone because I can't put up with this loneliness any longer." You can try to fool other people if you want to, but you can't fool yourself. You have to be honest with yourself and not pretend that you're so tough you don't need a mate. *If you're not honest with yourself, God can't show you the wonderful plan He has for your life.*

Category two is the single person who truly desires not to be married. There are some people who are single and have no desire to be married. They're not kidding; they're not playing games. They've made up their minds—marriage is not what they want. Maybe it's a matter of "Been there, done that." Maybe they've been married before and are now divorced. Maybe they've never been married, but they've been in relationships before and are not interested in another one. Marriage is not an issue for them. *If you're in this category, you shouldn't date.* Otherwise, you'll open yourself up to all kinds of temptations.

God's Approval

For people who do have a desire to become married, it's very important that your dating has God's approval. In order to decide if you do, ask yourself a few questions. Is God a part of our relationship? Is our relationship in the will of God? Has God placed this person in my life? Is this the individual whom God wants to pronounce His blessings over? Is this the individual I can commit myself to for the rest of my life? Can you visualize the minister placing his hands upon you both and saying, "...whom God has joined together, let no man put asunder"?

If you answered "yes" to those questions, you may have found that special someone you were designed to love. When you come to the point in your relationship where both of you agree that you love one another, your dating should move to the next level—the honorable stage of marriage. I don't encourage people to date too long. Let me clarify myself. I don't mean that you should try to determine whether or not someone should be your potential husband or wife after just one month of dating and then quickly get married. You can't know somebody well enough in one month or perhaps even in six months to say that you'll marry them. (Although the truth is, there will never be enough time to completely figure out another human being. When you think you know everything about an individual, they'll change on you in a split second. It keeps life interesting.) You need to take enough time to ensure that God wants the two of you joined together.

Marriage, an Honorable State

Those who are engaged to be married have to be especially careful. If you yield to the many temptations that the devil will put in your way, you will miss some of the blessings that God has for you. For you to have God's approval, you should keep away from all evil (I Thes 5:22). How? James 4:7 says to resist the devil, and he will flee from you. You should not lie to yourself that you can handle all the temptations encountered in any situation. You shouldn't think that you and your date can go anywhere you want to go because you both are strong and can withstand the temptations that you'll face. You shouldn't say, "I can go to my boyfriend's/girlfriend's house or other places that might tempt us, but we won't stray from the will of God and defile His temple. We're strong enough; we know that we can handle it." You're making a big mistake when you kid yourself and think you're strong enough to control your flesh under any circumstance. There's a powerful, God-given chemistry between a man and a woman that you have to be aware of.

Some people get married in order to use that chemistry and enjoy "legal" sex. If you get married just to partake of the sex you desire, you're making an enormous mistake. The sex act is not a continual thing, but your relationship *is*. You will have a relationship 24 hours a day, seven days a week for the rest of your life. If you do not truly love the other person, you will be cheating both of you out of God's blessings. So many people wish they could go back in time just a few years. They've come to realize that they made a wrong choice. If they knew then what they know now, things would be different.

The devil wants to use your body that God created to divide you from Him. He's like a roaring lion seeking whom he may devour. He operates within our flesh, making us think that we're tempted beyond that which we can endure, so we might as well give in. But God's Word teaches us important principles that will help us through temptation. He wants to bless us when we make the marriage covenant.

*How can your body glorify God?
First of all, make sure that
your spirit is stronger than the
appetites of your body. If you
can get your spirit to line up with
the Word of God, then it can
command your body to
follow its instructions,
and you won't succumb
to temptation.*

CHAPTER FOUR

Overcoming the Flesh

Flee fornication. Every sin that a man doeth is without the body; but he that committeth fornication sinneth against his own body.

What? know ye not that your body is the temple of the Holy Ghost which is in you, which ye have of God, and ye are not your own?

For ye are bought with a price: therefore glorify God in your body, and in your spirit, which are God's. (I Corinthians 6:18-20)

Beyond Passion

In the same way that God wants to use our bodies to glorify Him, the devil wants to use our bodies to exalt himself and denounce the power of God. As a single Christian, you need to understand that your body is a temple of the Holy Ghost. It should glorify God—with your lips you praise Him, with your hands you worship Him. With your whole body, your whole being, you should praise and glorify the Lord. If you unite your body with another person with whom you're not in marriage covenant, then God says that your body can't glorify Him until you seek forgiveness and become cleansed in the blood of Jesus. The devil works hard against singles because if he can get you to defile the temple, he has conquered you, at least for the time being.

Because it is God's temple, your body is more important to Him than your relationship to the person you love. You need to rethink whether or not you will continue the relationship because your body and spirit belong to God. The devil will come to you and suggest that you can "Go ahead and glorify God with your spirit, but don't worry about glorifying Him with your body except in church." The enemy will tell you that as long as you go to church and praise God, sing the hymns, and read the Scriptures, that's enough.

Overcoming the Flesh

How *can* your body glorify God? First of all, make sure that your spirit is stronger than the appetites of your body. If you can get your spirit to line up with the Word of God, then it can command your body to follow its instructions, and you won't succumb to temptation. Tell yourself, "I cannot defile the temple." When your temple is undefiled, you will walk in holiness and your body will glorify God.

Today people don't want to hear what God's Word says about the issue. They say, "There's no need for us to hold out and not have premarital sex as long as we know that we're going to get married some day." The church has gotten so liberal that it's unusual to hear abstinence preached. People only want to hear how God can deliver them, prosper them, and heal them. However, what God desires above all is to have people in His Church who walk in holiness.

Handling Temptations

Holiness is not an easy thing to come by. You must overcome temptations every day in order to attain it. Don't act as though you've never been tested by the devil on a date. One of the things that destroys us is that we are dishonest with ourselves.

As a single person, you need to be honest with yourself and with your date. Tell the person the truth. Once the movie is over, tell them that you need to go home, otherwise something may happen that you hadn't planned on happening and that would not be good. Be honest. As Christians, we act as though nothing is difficult for us. We think each of us is a superperson. When you say good night, just thank him, but don't linger with the door open. Once again, let the person know he can't come in because the two of you may be tempted beyond what you can handle. If you yield to temptation, you may feel good for a while, but in the end, you're going to feel sorry.

If you have fallen in this regard, God wants you to *start over*. God loves you so much, that even though you made a mistake, He desires to forgive you and give you another chance. Listen to the Word, so that the Word will change you and give you strength the next time you are faced with a temptation. If you are His child, it shouldn't be your desire to live a life of sin. You should want to glorify Him.

The devil will trip you up in the dating process if you aren't careful. You'll start doing things you've no business doing. But notice what the scripture says in I Corinthians 6:18: "flee fornication." Do you know what that word flee means? You should run for your life if you see the temptation coming because fornication defiles the temple of God.

Date for a while and get to know the person. From dating, you should progress to getting engaged. The engagement should lead to the wedding date. The process sounds simple, but I know in reality walking through all the temptations connected with it is tough.

Set Your Parameters

To protect yourself, set some parameters for your dating. *As a preacher*, I won't tell you that while you're dating you should never hold hands or hug. But I am telling you to *know your limits*. That's why it's so important to be honest with yourselves. Some people can hug, and because they're strong, they're okay. Some people can kiss to a certain degree, and because they're strong, they're okay. But there are some people who cannot even hold hands because they'll go beyond their limitation. They can hardly even look, much less touch, without strong temptation overtaking them!

How strong are you? Know how far you and your fiancé can go without being compelled to sin.

God wants us to keep our bodies pure. So do whatever it takes for you to keep your body pure. Your wedding day may be a year from now. In the meantime, if you have to lock yourself in the house to stay pure—do it. Think about limiting your number of dates per week and talk more to each other on the telephone. Whatever you have to do to keep your body pure—do it.

I know this is a word that is hard to swallow. You are probably saying, "God, we didn't expect all of this. This author is living back in the 50s. Who gets married today without already having sex?" You may say, "Well, I have to check the other person out before we get married—I have to see if they can perform." That's the very reason I stated before that if God is in it, do it His way, and everything is going to be fine. If you ask Him for a fish, do you think He'll give you a stone?

Fixing the Problem

God is aware of all your faults. Not only that, He knows how much you love Him. You made a decision never to turn your back on God. Your desire is to serve Him. The Lord knows that. But He *also knows* your weaknesses. He knows you're dating. Maybe you've been dating for years. Perhaps during that time you've entered a union that God can't bless because you haven't gotten married. God is saying, "I want to fix it. Let Me bless the union." If you say to yourself, "No, don't bless that one Lord. I have no intention of marrying that person," then go to that person and say, "I'm sorry for leading you on. I apologize for offending you, but I have to break off this relationship." Of course, more than likely they're going to become angry. You have to be honest with them because you want to do right in the sight of God. If they become angry, they'll eventually get over it. The relationship was a mistake in the first place, but now your conscience is clear.

It's best not to enter into another relationship until you know whether or not the person you'll be seeing is worthy of you. Dating was never meant to be a way to "try someone out." Dating was never intended to allow you to live as a common law husband and wife. Christians have no business living with anyone that they're not in covenant with. The Bible says if you're living with someone and not married, you need to get your clothes and run for your life. The Word is, "Flee."

God's plan and purpose for your life is very important. You should know your limits and stick within them when you're dating. Remember, it all boils down to one thing—God says He wants your body to be holy and to be set apart so you can glorify Him.

God knows that fulfilling your sexual desires will be enjoyable, but He also has decreed that this fulfillment should only take place in marriage. When you keep your bodies holy for the time when you make a marriage covenant, God's blessing will be upon your union.

CHAPTER FIVE

Keeping Your Body Holy

Now the works of the flesh are manifest, which are these; Adultery, fornication, uncleanness, lasciviousness (Galatians 5:19).

What is *lasciviousness*? According to the dictionary, lasciviousness is characterized by lust, lewd, and exciting sexual desires. Now this can be misleading. You may come to the conclusion that God says all sexual desire is wrong. On the contrary, God is the one who created us with sexual desires. The truth is that God has created an environment, called marriage, in which sexual desires can be legitimately fulfilled. That is the only way He allows you to explore your sexual desires.

In the 21st century, the prevailing attitude is, "I'm dating someone, and you don't expect me to have premarital sex? I can't believe it. That's old-fashioned!" Some singles are engaged in lasciviousness and commit the act of fornication, but God wants you to learn the plan He has for your life. He wants you to use your body to glorify Him rather than explore your sexual desires before the proper time of marriage. When your body explores sexual desires without the benefit of a marriage covenant, the only person who gets glorified is the devil.

You can see why it's dangerous for two people to be dating for a very long period of time. When you date for years, you'll have many more temptations to overcome. I'm not suggesting that you should date someone for just one month and then get married to them. I'm suggesting that first you pray and ask God to give you the right person. Listen to Him and He'll tell you if that man is yours or if that woman is yours. The moment the confirmation is in for both of you, then your dating should lead to an engagement and, shortly afterwards, marriage. Once God speaks to both of you that the one you're dating is the right person for you, what's holding you back from planning more than just where to go on the next date?

The Bible doesn't specifically put a limitation on the length of dating, but I think it's unwise for Christians to be in a dating relationship for several years. That gives way too much room for the devil to work.
Hebrews 13:4 says:

Marriage is honourable in all, and the bed undefiled; but whoremongers and adulterers God will judge.

Marriage is honorable and holy. But when you're dating, it's very important to refuse all wrong desires and works of the flesh. Wrong desires are like biological hand grenades. When two people come together and refuse to honor their limits, it's like pulling the pin on the grenade. As Christians living in the 21st century, we must fight daily to keep our bodies pure. God is not so much interested in whether you call yourself a Christian or are loyal to your church. Having all kinds of religious symbols in your house and car is also wonderful, but what's the point if you don't keep your body holy?

You need to be real with yourselves. For those who are single and have no desire to marry, there is no room for discussion here. If you've no desire to marry, the subject of dating is closed. Stay by yourself. If anyone approaches you, tell them you're not interested in dating. It's just as simple as that. Don't beat around the bush. However, if you are interested in getting married, there are things you should learn to do. There are limitations you'll need to recognize. Eve stood before the serpent and had no desire to sin. But the serpent had a good line prepared for her, so she listened to him and not to what God had told her. She was deceived by not following the limitations God put on her.

Recognizing Your Limitations

You and your fiancé may have a conversation that goes something like this: "Well, we know last weekend the sermon was about premarital sex, but I want to express myself completely to you. I have never felt this way about another person in my entire life." You must respond, "I appreciate that, but we need to keep our bodies pure."

The devil's intention is to destroy you by tempting you to defile your body. He pushes you to the extreme and before you know it, you say,

"Okay, all right. Since you're not going to go to bed with me, can I get a good night kiss?" Is kissing wrong? No, it's not wrong. However, there are limitations to kissing. If you push the other person too far, you can easily end up doing the one thing that you have vowed not to do. You will disappoint God and each other because you didn't wait.

The devil may begin his onslaught in a very innocent way. He may suggest that the man should buy the woman flowers. Women are very sensitive to things like flowers. When you buy a woman flowers, she says, "Oh, you shouldn't have," which really means, "You should have!" However, the devil can twist something that should be a blessing into something that is a temptation. How? He will tempt you to buy something that will touch her heart in order to entice her to let you into her apartment. She told you not to come over because she was alone. But, you allow your desire for her to rule you, and you use flowers as a way to get what you want. Woman, if he knocks on your door with flowers, know your limitations. Don't open the door. *But he came all this way. I couldn't do that. Just let me open the door and take the flowers and shut it back.* It's really not a wise thing to do. There's a good possibility that you may get yourself into trouble! Maybe you'll just have to take a pass on those flowers this time. It goes beyond him; it goes beyond the flowers; it has to do with being strong enough to know your limitations in order to keep your body holy.

You need to know your limitations because a biological hand grenade can destroy you. It starts out with natural appetites. When you meet somebody of the opposite sex, there's an attraction. You begin to love that person. God is all for it—He's in your cheering section—because it's leading to marriage. That's wonderful. You start out with just holding hands, and you feel okay. Next you start to hug. That's fine too. But before you know it, you're hugging with a more intense affection. Your bodies are pressed together. Then touching sensitive parts of the body becomes a part of your relationship. What makes you think that the other person is not going to react? You say, "We can handle that; we're strong; we're okay." Then you kiss on the cheek. That's fine. But then you progress to lip kissing. Finally it involves the hands, lips, and body pressed together touching each other. Before you know it, you've moved to the climax of the moment, which is intercourse.

Singles be honest. If you have sex, don't you feel

guilty afterwards? God loves you, and He wants you to change. God is coming to you in a loving way saying, "You think I didn't see you, but I saw what you did last night. But, I love you and long to see you choose My way." You are both Christians. Keep your bodies holy and let your dating lead to marriage. He will honor that relationship.

Whatever it takes to avoid fornication, do it. If it means telling your date, "I live alone, and you can't come over to my house," just do it. If he talks about going to the movies together where the lights are low knowing this is your weak spot, just say, "You know, let's do something else instead." Whatever you have to do to keep your body pure, then for heaven's sake, do it. You're really helping each other. And God will be pleased.

Reasons to Wait

There are reasons why God has commanded us to wait until marriage to fulfill our sexual desires. Waiting controls your desires. Controlling your desires puts them under subjection. The risk in not waiting is that you'll be driven by lust. Help your body to wait. Maybe the prayer you need to pray is not for a wife or husband. Maybe your prayer should be, "Lord sanctify me. Help me to wait." On the night of your honeymoon, the joyful result of waiting when God pronounces a blessing over your union is a wonderful experience. You can now explore each other to your hearts' content. God will smile down on you and declare that your bed is not defiled.

Your kids will pattern themselves after you, and they will see a good role model. When kids see a single parent living with someone, they know something immoral is going on. Kids are smart. It will lead them to think, *This is okay. I can take my body and do whatever I want with it.* God says, "No, the body I have given you is My temple. You must keep it holy."

God loves you and knows it is a difficult world in which you live. If you're a Christian and are dating, first of all make sure you're dating a Christian. If you're a Christian and your fiancé is not, you're about to embark on a rocky road at best. If you're dating someone who is not a Christian, you better decide to call that person and end the relationship right away. Let nonbelievers date nonbelievers, and let believers date believers.

If you're unmarried and living with a believer, be honest. You're the salt of the earth. You're the light of the world. How can you show this dark world what God stands for when you're practicing the very thing that He denounced? If you're living with someone, move out *now*. Let them know you have some house cleaning to do. Tell them you're not going to become physically joined any more until the two of you say, "I do." Now if the other person decides not to marry you, that's fine. Tell them, "As much as I want to do it, as much as my flesh leads me to do it, I'm cutting off this sin. When I go to church next Sunday, I don't want to feel like I felt last Sunday. I want to bring glory to God."

God knows that fulfilling your sexual desires will be enjoyable, but He also has decreed that this fulfillment should only take place in marriage. When you keep your bodies holy for the time when you make a marriage covenant, God's blessing will be upon your union.

We should never use sex as a motive for getting two people to become husband and wife. We should use the love that Christ speaks about. If they do not love each other, sex cannot keep them together forever. We may find out after they have gotten married that they really didn't love each other.

Chapter Six

Temptations of the Flesh

And when he was at the place, he said unto them, pray that ye enter not into temptation.

And he was withdrawn from them about a stone's cast, and kneeled down, and prayed,

Saying, Father, if thou be willing, remove this cup from me; nevertheless not my will, but thine, be done. (Luke 22:40-42)

This prayer expresses how Jesus felt when He knew He was going to be crucified. The thought of the anticipated arrest and public disgrace was the most difficult situation He had ever faced. I believe at that very moment Jesus must have been tempted to flee. Thoughts like this probably filtered through His mind: "I am going to be put to disgrace. My flesh is going to suffer. So the best thing to do is get out of this situation."

In verse 42 Jesus said, "If Thou be willing, remove this cup from Me; nevertheless not My will, but Thine be done." Here we see Jesus praying to His Father something like this, "If the tempting of My flesh brings You glory, so let it be. I am willing. Even though My flesh is going to suffer, even though I will be put in the most difficult position of My ministry and My life, I'm willing to go through it because it was divinely designed for the good."

Jesus did not willingly experience temptation in order to get selfish gain from it or so that His flesh would be rewarded. The cross was the plan of His Father. God the Father divinely ordained that Jesus was going to be arrested by the soldiers and crucified for the salvation of the world. He wanted the entire world to see that Jesus actually had become flesh, lived with us, and provided the way for us so that we, too, can conquer the flesh.

Key to Overcoming

At the beginning of His ministry, Jesus was tested by the devil in the desert. He used the Word to conquer temptation when He said, "It is written..." If single people will follow the pattern of Jesus, they will be successful in denying temptation. Everyone is tempted, but God provides His Word to help you resist temptation. It is God's will that when you experience temptations that you stand firm as Jesus did and not succumb to the wiles of the enemy.

Jesus didn't walk around the streets of Jerusalem, Samaria, and Judea and willingly create an environment that would test His faith. He didn't look for situations that would make Him vulnerable. Let's look at the story of the Samaritan woman at the well. Jesus knew that the woman there was divinely appointed to meet Him. When they talked, Jesus kept his conversation focused. He used the natural things of life to share with the woman a spiritual revelation. Jesus didn't willingly put himself in a position of temptation by saying things such as, "Your body is very attractive." He didn't do that because that statement would create an environment that could stimulate the flesh to lust. Neither should we put ourselves in situations that will test our ability to withstand temptation.

Singles need to understand that when you go out into the world, your light has to shine. You bring the light of Jesus Christ into this dark world. You have to live your life in such a way that when the world looks at you, it can see a difference. It's only when you walk through your life with a clear conscience that you can speak Jesus' words to others. He didn't compliment the woman on her dress or how she looked, although she must have been very attractive since so many men had married her. There had to be something special about this woman to have that many lovers. But my point is that Jesus did not make himself vulnerable to the flesh and put Himself in a position where the flesh could overpower Him. Instead, He shared with her about her spiritual condition.

Avoid Temptation

Singles need to understand that they should never allow themselves to be forced into temptation. Many times you create your own temptations by willingly going into situations that are wrong for you to be in. When you get into them, you realize that they're beyond your control, but you continue anyway and allow the flesh to lead you.

Society today declares that you're an adult and you shouldn't let anyone dictate how to live your life. Freedom is wonderful, but you should let the Word of God be your guide. God's Word should instruct you on how to live your life. It has to be the compass that gives you clear direction to where God wants you to go.

If you're a single person living by yourself, and you invite your fiancé over, you have now created an environment that will tempt your flesh to take control over your spirit. You may ask how do you deal with the need to have moments alone with your fiancé. The Bible teaches us that we must shun the very appearance of evil. Anything that looks like it's going to create evil or cause you to disobey God must be avoided. Don't allow room for it. Don't give into it. One way to address this need for some privacy is to be alone in a room with family or friends in the next room. What you especially should be careful of is make sure you and your fiancé are in an environment where the flesh will not be tempted to control you.

I don't want to tell you how you should live your life. And I really don't want to go back to the traditional way where leaders prescribed rules for dating that were not biblical. Although some of these rules kept the singles in line, they were outside the will of God. Any rules and regulations not in the will of

God are not pleasing to Him. There is one blanket instruction, however, that holds true for anyone in any situation: You need to make sure that if God were to step into your situation, He would be pleased about what you are doing, and it would bring glory to Him.

I counseled a young couple who were dating. The young lady came to me and said that she was having a difficult time in the relationship. She thought he was wonderful, and they were both putting some cash into a savings account so that one day they could get married. No wedding date was set. Her major concern was that they were committing the act of fornication. She asked me how she could change the situation. She said they were really in love but not ready to get married for at least a year. She admitted that 12 months of waiting seemed too long. "I'm attracted to him," she said. "Sometimes the situation we're in just moves us from one level of showing affection to the next. We'll go to a movie together, and from the movie we'll drive in the car to the next place we're going. But in the car, we'll start kissing. The kissing will lead to petting, and then before we hardly know it, we've gone all the way." She asked what she could do in order to overcome this temptation. I asked

Temptations of the Flesh

her a couple of questions and was not surprised at her answers.

I asked her first of all about her spiritual life—how often she prayed, went to church, and studied her Bible. And then I asked her, "Do you and your fiancé have weekly Bible study where you sit and read the Bible and deal with scriptures that pertain to your circumstances—how to deal with temptation, how to deal with sexual sins and so forth? Do you go to religious meetings such as singles' conferences that will help you to develop stronger faith in your life?

Her answers easily explained why she was not able to resist the devil. The couple attended church once a week at the most. They went to one Sunday service, had lunch together, and then took in a movie or drove to the beach. They very seldom attended a Bible study because of work or other reasons. On the other hand, they often went to the mall and shopped. Sometimes he went to her place and other times she went to his place. It was obvious to me that they were entertaining the enemy and giving him room to work in their lives instead of building up their faith. They were not at a place where they could see God at work in their lives. They were feeding the flesh more than the spirit man.

Beyond Passion

"When you go to the mall, what kind of clothes do you buy?" I asked her. She started describing the clothes. I said, "You're buying clothes that will make yourself appealing to him. Whether they're revealing clothes or not, what you're doing is feeding the flesh with thoughts about your body. You can counteract that train of thought by giving some of the money you're spending at the mall to some charitable Christian organization. Pour the finances in there and say 'Lord, bless this ministry and open doors for them.' I don't mean that you shouldn't buy clothes and make yourself attractive to him. What I'm saying is when your main focus is trying to appeal to the other person, that opens the door for the enemy to come in and use that very thing against you."

I showed her the various reasons she was struggling with temptation. I explained that if they were not going to church, they were not allowing the Word of God to nourish them. If they made a decision to get into the Word of God, what they studied would easily come to their minds when they were tempted. They could use it against the enemy just as Jesus did against Satan's temptation.

Finally I said to her, "There's nothing wrong with going to the movies or attending various social events. But if you go more often to secular social events that feed the mind, work on the emotions, and make you dwell on the flesh, then you'll weaken the spirit man. You should increase the amount of time that you feed your relationship with the Word of God. You need to find some singles' conferences or seminars to attend. You can go to the movies, but you shouldn't go to the movies more often than you go to church. Going to the movies three times in a week and to church only once is totally out of balance. You must make sure the weight of the power and the Word of God in your life is much heavier than that of the flesh. If you keep doing that, you'll find that the Word of God will be more powerful in your life than the flesh."

I shared with her that they needed to start changing their way of life not only by going to events that feed the spirit man, but also by reading books that do the same thing. They needed to direct a large portion of their conversations around the Bible. I told her that if they would stay in the Word, their lives would be totally changed.

What I tried to do was redeem the situation with this couple for the Lord. In the past, when people came for counseling, many times they were told to marry right away so they would not continue to sin. Church leaders, and Christians in general, sometimes rush people who are dating into marriage to keep them holy, pure, and away from sexual sins. I believe that it's against God's will to force people into marriage because they want to have sex. We should never use sex as a motive for getting two people to become husband and wife. We should use the love that Christ speaks about. If they do not love each other, sex cannot keep them together forever. We may find out after they have gotten married that they really didn't love each other. What they experienced before was only lustful attraction, and so by forcing them to marry quickly we have created a dilemma—do they live a lie or do they divorce each other? Either one should be unacceptable. So it becomes difficult for these singles, and eventually they don't want to trust God anymore. They feel the Christian journey is not for them.

The better way is for them to find out in the beginning whether God has truly brought the two of them together. If so, they know they can depend on His grace to help them and His Word to guide them so they can much better resist temptation.

Singles need to know how to reject temptations that other people present to them. When someone comes and proposes something to you that is not of God, you should be bold enough to stand up and say, "I'm sorry, I may offend you, but I'm not going to give in to this."

CHAPTER SEVEN

Dealing With Temptation

How do you deal with temptation? That question is the most common one singles ask when they go for counseling. How do you overcome the flesh?

Stand fast therefore in the liberty where with Christ hath made us free, and be not entangled again with the yoke of bondage. (Galatians 5:1)

The apostle Paul encouraged the Church to stand fast in Jesus Christ and in the truth that God has revealed to us through His Word and be free of the yoke of the enemy. In order to overcome the difficult temptations they face and be free to truly enjoy this time in their lives, singles need to spend time in the Word. Nine times out of ten when you talk to singles who are struggling with temptation, you'll find they have more of the world or the flesh and less of the Word in them.

The Bible tells us that the Word is quick, sharp, and powerful. You need to understand that you *will be* tempted. The moment you're tempted, remembering the Word will empower you to overcome the temptation. But God can't bring something to your remembrance that you've never read.

Say, for instance, you have an examination coming up but instead of studying for it, you hang out with your friends. The next day you shouldn't go to the exam room and pray for the ability to pass the test. That's ridiculous. You study first, then you pray and ask God to give you the ability to do your best. When it comes to temptation, one of the most effective ways to deal with it is to study the Word. Take time out on a daily basis to read the Scriptures. Study the Word, and you'll be successful in the testings that inevitably come.

Situations Faced by Singles

Singles need to know how to reject temptations that other people present to them. When someone comes and proposes something to you that is not of God, you should be bold enough to stand up and say, "I'm sorry, I may offend you, but I'm not going to give in to this." When you make that declaration, the enemy will flee from you. Standing your ground without any apology or hesitation is an effective way of dealing with the tempter. The enemy is defeated, but don't be surprised if he comes back later and tests you once again.

A person may come to you and say, "I've been going out with you for three weeks now and, you know, I really think it's time that you and I enter into a sexual relationship." Right up front in a very Christian manner you should respond, "Well, maybe that's what you want, but I'm going to stand my ground. I will not defile the temple of the Holy Spirit."

When men face situations where females present their bodies in a revealing way, men ought to stand up and say, "You know, I care about you. In order for me to keep my right standing with God, and if we're going to continue our relationship, the presentation of your image has to be different. I don't mean any offense, but I'm saying this for our good." You have to show firmness. If there is no firmness, then you are not effectively dealing with the temptation. No one plays with fire without getting burned. No one willingly places their hand in a fire because they know what the end result will be.

It's the same thing in our spiritual walk. If we catch the enemy trying to entice us to walk outside the will of God, we need to immediately confront the issue and declare that we're not going to yield to it. We should say, "It's written that this is against the will of God, and I'm going to please God. I'm going to walk in the will of God. I'm not going to lower myself to the lust of the flesh. The lust of the flesh will cause me to hurt God. I love Him and I'm not going to do that. I love you, too, but I love God more." That's tough to say. It's even tougher for someone to hear. But if you are firm, God will give you the ability to overcome the challenges that you have in your daily walk.

Compatible Goals

Another way of dealing with temptations of the flesh when you're dating is to look for compatible goals. We're all created by God in various unique ways. You're different from me, and I'm different from you. However, there must be some common goals that the two of you can agree upon so that you will be able to function together in harmony.

If you're dating and you discover that your fiancé is a person whose flesh is weak, and you know that you're the same, be careful! I'm not trying to tell you not to date him. What I am saying is that if you set up guidelines in dating someone, you should come to a mutual understanding about them. The Bible asks how can two walk together except they agree? How can light and darkness be in the same place at the same time? It doesn't work. You need a fiancé who has a like spirit so that you can work together toward the same goals, then after you're married, you'll be able to live together compatibly.

If you have a fiancé who always wants to engage in sexual acts with you and you're both Christians, it's not going to work. If you're trying to stay in the Word and he's not into the Word, it's not going to work. Someone is going to have to give in. There is going to be a conflict if one enjoys the things of the world much more than the other. One day, the relationship will probably explode.

Singles need to find companions who have like

spirits where they're both willing to attend church together, and they're both there to stay focused. This focus will help you deal with temptation. When the tempter comes, both of you will be able to agree to resist him and will support each other instead of engaging in arguments.

Regular Counseling

The next practice in dealing with temptation is for singles to agree to get regular *counseling*. Do not try to do it by yourself. There are great women and men of God who can deposit years of experience into your life. Some singles, and especially young ones, try to learn by trial and error. They find out soon enough that there is a big price to pay when they attempt to learn without using the experience of experts. So many singles find that when the tempter comes, they aren't able to overpower him because they shut themselves off from the wisdom of the elders. When I talk about the elders, I'm talking about older people who have "been there, done that." When singles who ignore helpful advice fall into temptation and have intercourse, they sometimes then will finally seek counseling. They could have avoided the pain that comes from the fruit of their sin by going for counseling in the first place.

Dealing With Temptation

Let me share the story of a particular lady who would not listen to the elders. Older family members tried to tell her that a certain gentleman was not really good for her. (I've learned over the years that people who are older than I am will say things that I may not at first agree with. But if I listen carefully to their years of experience, I learn wisdom that helps me to become a better person.)

This young lady told me she didn't listen to her elders, and it so happened she conceived and had a child by the young man they had warned her about. She soon found out that he was having other affairs outside of their relationship, so she didn't want to marry him. She made a decision to get her life straightened out and become the young woman that God wanted her to be. But she had a big problem—she wanted him out of her life, but he didn't want to go. All she wanted him to do was to support his child. However, he's a very controlling person, and he didn't want her or the child to leave him.

She was now in a very difficult position. She wanted to get her life right. She wanted to do the right thing, but this man continued to give her problems even when they were no longer living together. Because of her sin (fornication) and because she didn't listen to her elders, she will now have the challenging task of raising her child alone and also arranging visits for him with the father. When there is a child involved, it's not the same as with someone who can walk away with no strings attached. The father has every legal right to have contact with his child, and she will have to deal with visitation rights until the child turns 18.

Singles can greatly benefit from the elders' counsel in the decisions they make. They especially need to get counseling from people who can show them the difference between the real and the fake. What may look wonderful, may not be so wonderful. What may look like gold, may not be gold. What may look like it's flourishing may be a deception. Your relationship may look good. You think he/she loves you, but when you hear the elders say to you that there is something strange about that young man/woman, stop a minute. Before you put up a wall to block out what they're saying, examine the situation. See why they're telling you to beware of your date. You may find out that it won't hurt you to slow down and let God reveal His perfect will for your life.

Avoid "No Future" Relationships

Avoid long-term relationships that have no future. These relationships are entered into by people who date with no intention of getting married. We saw earlier how dating is really not an option for them. They don't want to settle down and move from the dating position into the honorable marriage position. But God didn't create intimacy for you to enjoy for just a season. It's the same with your intimacy with God. He wants you to *stay* in His presence. When you go into a relationship with no intention of getting married, it's very dangerous. You probably won't be able to avoid temptation, and the relationship is nothing you can build upon for your future.

As I said before, you shouldn't rush out and get married just to legalize sex. You must be thinking about the future when you start dating and come to know whether or not this is the person you want to settle down with. After a period of time, there ought to be a commitment to become husband and wife to honor and glorify God. After the marriage has been sealed, you can become one and the bed will be undefiled. God will be glorified. There will be no spirit of disobedience. There will be no spirit of the enemy or the flesh controlling your relationship.

When God placed Adam and Eve in the garden, their union was put together by God and He gave them freedom. With that freedom he said to them, "Everything in this garden you can have, but there is one tree you should not touch." God has given you the ability to date, to care for each other, and to love each other, but there is one forbidden fruit in a dating relationship you should not touch and that is sex. Adam and Eve sinned because they listened to the enemy and submitted to him. You must desire to bring yourselves to the Lord for His blessing, or you're opening yourself up to the schemes of the enemy to use your flesh to conquer the will of God in your life.

The pressures in today's world to eat of the forbidden fruit are enormous for singles. The next five chapters will deal with pressures that singles in particular have to face and how to handle them.

Both men and women are sensitive to what society says to them. Instead, they should be sensitive to what God says to them. They should be careful to use the Word as their guide instead of the latest advertising trends.

CHAPTER EIGHT

Pressures That Singles Have to Deal With

And we know that all things work together for good to them that love God, to them who are the called according to his purpose.

For whom he did foreknow, he also did predestinate to be conformed to the image of his Son, that he might be the firstborn among many brethren.

He that spared not his own Son, but delivered him up for us all, how shall he not with him also freely give us all things?

Who shall lay any thing to the charge of God's elect? It is God that justifieth.

Who is he that condemneth? It is Christ that died, yea rather, that is risen again, who is even at the right hand of God, who also maketh intercession for us.

Who shall separate us from the love of Christ? shall tribulation, or distress, or persecution, or famine, or nakedness, or peril, or sword? (Rom. 8:28-29; 32-35)

If none of the difficulties listed above can separate us from the love of God, then with God's grace, singles can handle the pressures of singles we'll deal with in the next several chapters. The five pressures are: society, loneliness and isolation, sexual pleasure, parenting, and insufficiency. In talking about these pressures, we will deal with some practical issues. I believe if singles can successfully deal with these five difficulties, they'll be able to have a fulfilling relationship.

Pressure From Society

Society puts pressure on all of us to become what they have become. For men, one of the pressures is to *impress*. Men will go out of their way to write a poem for their fiancée because women are moved by it. Single men will even tell lies to impress a woman. They may say things such as, "You look so gorgeous tonight" even though they may hate the outfit you're wearing. But because they want to get their way, they'll try to impress you. They're pressured to impress.

Men try to impress women with their *physique*. We know that women admire well-built men. If a woman sees an Arnold Schwarzenegger with big muscles on one side of the street and a 90 pound skinny man on the other side of the street, which one will she be attracted to? More than likely it will be Arnold because he has a terrific physique. Many men feel obligated to maintain what they think a woman wants. They'll go to the gym and work out because they feel compelled to impress single women.

Men impress with their *cars*. There are a lot of women who are in awe of a man who drives a fancy car such as a Mercedes or BMW. The man could be broke and ugly, but let him drive up in a Porsche and some women want to get his number. A lot of men know they can drive down the street in their fancy car, and women will look at them. They feel confident that their car will open the doors to conversation with beautiful women.

Men impress with their *appearance*. Many men wear the finest clothes and jewelry. Whenever you see them, they're always wearing the latest fashion. They are "pretty boys" without any money. Most of them still live with Momma. Society pressures men to live that way. They are told by all the commercials and ads that they have to dress expensively to impress a woman.

While a man is single, he should save his money so that when he marries a woman, he has enough to buy a house and take care of the kids if she gets pregnant right away. He shouldn't get caught up in what marketing people have cleverly packaged as reality. He shouldn't be forced by society to buy a car or an expensive suit that he can't afford just to impress her. Then when he gets married, he might not have any assets or money saved at all.

You may ask how does the scripture in Romans relate to all of this? Verse 32 says, "He that spared not his own Son, but delivered him up for us all, how shall he not with him also freely give us all things?" Women, why would you allow your man to be so pressured to impress you with a car or other material things? If you humble yourself, God will give you the right man *first* and the fancy car *later* in the right season. God will freely give things to you at the proper time.

I recently read a book entitled *The Millionaire Next Door* by Dr. Thomas Stanley and Dr. William Danko. It states that most people in America who have a lot of money don't spend it the way the average American spends their money. Unfortunately, because they're trying to impress women, a large portion of men have cars they can't afford.

If I were to sit down with some Christian men today who look good on the outside, and ask them to list their assets, I can guess what the answer will be. Do you have a house? No. Is your car paid off? No. Do you have a bank account? No. Do you have life insurance? No. Do you have a 401K? No. They may look good on the outside, but they have no assets. A woman would be crazy to date a man who looks good and drives a fancy car rather than one who may not wear the latest clothes or drive the fanciest car, but has substantial assets. No wonder when they get married, their marriage is in a terrible mess right away. They didn't realize that they can't live on looks alone.

Women need someone who will pay the rent. It's better to marry a not-so-attractive man with assets than a pretty boy with no assets. At least you know you'll be able to sleep at night because your bills will be paid. If he dies, you'll receive his insurance money and still be taken care of. Someone with no assets and no insurance will only leave you with a pile of bills.

Society Puts Pressure on Women

Women also feel pressure to be *attractive* in the same way that men do. A woman might buy $200 worth of cosmetics, clothes and jewelry, but leave her $40 light bill unpaid. A woman can put a weave on for $200, but not pay her $95 car insurance. Now, if you have a car accident and hit someone, would you rather go to jail looking pretty, or have the insurance company pay the bills? Isn't it better to pay your bills than try to impress society?

Some women who are single have *children to take care of*. Having children definitely presents a number of pressures. But if you re-examine your situation and set your priorities, life can be much easier. If you're in that situation you're probably not wealthy yet, so there are certain things you can't afford to do. As with men, society pressures you to dress in the latest style, putting a strain on your budget. Many women spend money on things they don't need. Then they come to church, and instead of praising God and thanking Him for giving them health and strength, their main focus in the worship service is: "God, give me a word tonight that will help me to be encouraged. God, I'm just about broke. I can't pay my rent, my telephone bill is due, my car note and insurance are due." The whole worship atmosphere is occupied with, "God, how can I get myself out of this?" God tried to warn you before, but you wouldn't listen. You let yourself be pressured into thinking that you had to look cute for Tommy. But if Tommy can't like you for who you are, you probably don't need him.

Society puts pressure on women *to be married by a certain age*. If you aren't married, something is supposedly wrong with you. In the same way, there's pressure for you to have children. If you're married for a year, people start to ask why you don't have any children yet. Then if you begin to have a number of children, society asks when are you going to stop! You can't win when you listen to society.

Both men and women are sensitive to what society says to them. *Instead, they should be sensitive to what God says to them.* They should be careful to use the Word as their guide instead of the latest advertising trends.

Beyond Passion

Don't build so many walls to protect yourself. Open up and learn to trust people. There are some strange people on this earth, but you don't have to be friends with everyone. If someone hurts you badly, end the relationship. But don't let it cut you off from everyone else.

CHAPTER NINE
Loneliness and Isolation

The second set of pressures affecting singles' relationships is loneliness and isolation. Genesis 2:18 says,

> *And the Lord God said, It is not good that the man should be alone; I will make him a help meet for him.*

From the very foundation of the world, God saw that it was not good for man to be alone. Of course when this scripture was written, it was specifically talking about the male gender. But I'm talking about both male and female. God saw it was not good for any of us to be alone. If God looked at us and noticed that we needed a companion, why then are we trying to isolate ourselves from each other? If God saw that we were lonely and needed someone, why do you pretend that it doesn't apply to you? If you're married, why do you try to isolate yourself from the person God has joined you to?

Isolation is one of the most destructive elements in a relationship. What isolation does is put you in a position where you create your own world. Many people build walls to protect themselves because they were hurt by people in the past. Some single people will say, "Forget it. It's been six months, a year, two years, and I haven't dated anybody. I'm not interested. Forget it." Some people have gone to the extreme and publicly said, "Even if the Lord Jesus Christ were to come and speak to me, I would still not be interested in marriage."

Do you know how dangerous a statement like that is? You're saying, "Even if God tells me to my face that marriage is what He wants for my life, I will tell Him that I'm not listening." The reason behind this attitude is probably that someone hurt you in the past. Instead, you should let your past experiences help you become better at choosing your mate in the next relationship. You now have a

Loneliness and Isolation

wealth of experience to help you in the next relationship. You'll know the red flags you should be aware of when someone wants to begin a relationship with you.

You're fearful of what people may say or do to you because you're trying to protect your future. What do I mean by that? Perhaps in the past you had shared your plans with someone and then that person betrayed you. Now you don't feel that you can trust anyone with your plans because maybe they will hurt you too.

Say for example you bought a car and your girlfriend all of a sudden became jealous and started rumors about you. Then some people began to shun you because of the lies your girlfriend told them. That incident caused you to put up protective walls and isolate yourself so no one could hurt you again. Now you've decided to buy a house. God has blessed you, and you're able to buy one for $200,000, but you decide not to share the information with anyone. You don't even want people to visit because of what happened in the past.

Now you may be saying, "If my friend got jealous over my car, how is she going to react to my new house?" It's a nice place, and you've fixed it up, but you never have any visitors. I'm not saying everyone should come to your house. (You'd be crazy to bring everyone there.) But don't say there isn't at least one person that God can help you trust so that you can invite them over. Most people will likely be happy that you have such a nice house. Why would you work for 30 years of your life to pay for that beautiful home and furniture, and not let anyone in the world enjoy it but you?

Don't build so many walls to protect yourself. Open up and learn to trust people. There *are* some strange people on this earth, but you don't have to be friends with everyone. If someone hurts you badly, end the relationship. *But don't let it cut you off from everyone else.*

In the news the other day, there was a story about an FBI agent who passed information to Russia. The interviewer asked another retired FBI agent if he thought the department would ever get to the place where a situation like this could not happen again. The former FBI agent said that as long as people are in any institution, system, or organization, it's open to betrayal like this. Man makes rules, and man can break them.

We're human beings. If someone hurts us, we

need to use the experience to help us select new friends. We need to look for certain qualities in a person based on past experiences. Hopefully we have learned to watch out for certain patterns of behavior that should be avoided. If someone walks into your house, you should expect to receive some type of pleasant response: "Congratulations, this is a nice place. I'm so happy for you. You did this by yourself? Bless you. I rejoice over your success." That person is saying I love what I see. I am not envious, I am happy for you."

On the other hand there can be negative responses that are best to avoid. Say for instance you get a new car. You would expect someone to say: "I love your car. Maybe one of these days you could give me a ride." But if they respond, "It's okay, but where are you going to get the money to pay for it?" Experience tells you to cut the conversation short, say your goodbyes, and drive off.

The final reason we choose to be isolated is the fact that we ourselves are self-centered and judgmental. We have become perfectionists and think we are the only ones who can do anything right. Because no one else is perfect like us, we create a wall and judge everyone else's efforts. This will cause us to build walls that can trap us into our own destructive dream world.

Beyond Passion

*You have to fight to keep
your bodies pure and holy before
God. It's a battle every day.
There are sexual desires in your
body that God has created,
but how do you express your
love toward the opposite
sex and still maintain your
Christian standards?
It's difficult.*

CHAPTER TEN

Sexual Pressure

The third pressure singles have to deal with is one of the most difficult things in a single (or married) relationship—*sexual pressure*. It is especially difficult for singles. You have to fight to keep your bodies pure and holy before God. It's a battle every day. There are sexual desires in your body that God has created, but how do you express your love toward the opposite sex and still maintain your Christian standards? It's difficult.

Oftentimes people who are single will struggle, and because they're so weak, they can't seem to resist the devil and end up engaging in intercourse.

Beyond Passion

Then ironically when a lot of these same couples get married, the thing they were struggling with before they got married, is something they *don't* want to do afterwards.

Many men have argued with their wife about being sexually fulfilled. "What's up? What's wrong with me? Is something wrong?" Men's sexual time schedules are totally different from women's. Some wives think having sex four times a month is enough. On the other hand, men feel it should be more like four times a week. The very thing God created for the holiness of marriage, is the very thing many of us are still warring about afterwards.

Single people are struggling *not to do* it, and married people are struggling *to do* it. For married people, sometimes it's an argument in the home that keeps the husband and wife apart. One little incident can create a mountain of a problem later. It can lead to disagreements with the children. Then when men are angry about their lack of sexual fulfillment, they filter it into other areas of their relationship. They don't empty the garbage, wash the car, or drop off the kids. They just shut down their contribution to the relationship.

Married people's sexual pressures are different

Sexual Pressure

than singles. Most singles suffer with how to live a holy life before God and keep sexual pressures out of it. Singles are in the position of dating someone they have a sexual appetite for. Is that wrong? No, it's natural. God gave you those appetites. As a man and woman you like each other. Some people may say holding hands when you're single is wrong. No, it's not wrong. You can hold hands. What is wrong with holding hands? What singles forget is something called *ground level*. Anytime you lift your feet off the ground, you're escalating the temptation. You're beginning to climb up the steps. You move up the step from holding hands to putting your arms around each other. Now you're not on ground level anymore. The moment your hands begin to touch another person who has a human sexual appetite for you, you have moved up another step.

You might say, "God understands that I love my partner. I'm hugging him, and he's hugging me. We're holding hands. What's the big deal? We haven't gone all the way." But the tone is set—the lights are dim. It's difficult to hold hands, hug each other, then back away and say "God bless you. I'll see you tomorrow." It's difficult to take the initiative and say, "I tell you what, it's time to read the Word." If you don't change the tone of the evening, you're giving the devil an opportunity to wreak havoc on your relationship.

Here is what usually happens. You go from having your arms around each other to light kissing. There's nothing wrong with that. But then you go to lingering kissing. From lingering kissing, you begin heavy necking. Do you see how dangerous this is now? It moves from heavy necking to light petting. The room begins to get hotter and hotter. Before you know it, BAM! All your resolve to have your relationship remain holy is over. It's history. The Holy Spirit says, "I want you to enjoy it. I created it for you. I want you to hug each other. I want you to have intercourse, but it is not the right time." Will you miss what the Holy Spirit desires to do in your relationship? Waiting for the proper time will bring blessing and honor to your future marriage.

*Take stock of where your
kids are and don't leap into
marriage just to alleviate
a problem. Let God lead
you into a marriage so
that He can bless it and help
you with all of the adjustments
that your family will
need to make along
the way.*

CHAPTER ELEVEN
Parenting

The fourth pressure singles have to deal with applies to those with children—the pressures related to parenting. How do you parent a child when you're a single mother or father? Emotionally and physically, how can you give support to your child/children? How can you provide financially for them? It's a difficult situation.

A lot of singles are dealing with the pressures of this issue. They don't know how to handle their children, and so they feel stressed all the time. Because they have children, they become very vulnerable. It's hard for them to make ends meet. Sometimes they need a supplementary income.

Society makes them think that if they have kids out of wedlock, no one is going to want to marry them. That's not true. There is hope for your future; God can provide a spouse who would love your children as their own.

Parenting is difficult, especially for single mothers. When you have boys, there comes a time in a boy's life when he wants to rap with a man. Women have a difficult time when the school says they're going to have camp and want the father to come camping with the son. Women don't know what to do.

Imagine how hard it is for a single father dealing with his daughter. The girl gets to a certain age when she is developing. Certain things are beginning to happen to her, and he cannot relate to them. Those of you who are going through parenting know how hard it is. Two are better than one. If you had a spouse, it would be so much better because there are certain things he or she could do, and certain things you can do that make a significant difference in the lives of children.

Another pressure that divorced single parents have is that they don't want to make mistakes with their children. They know that the kids are watching them carefully. If daddy leaves home, and he was the authoritative figure in the house, it becomes difficult for the mother to maintain discipline alone. She may have spoiled them in the past, but now she is the sole authoritative figure. She may have trouble controlling them. The child may begin to speak back to her and ignore the rules she has set for them. Their grades may even go down. Some single parents are working two jobs and don't have time to help them with their homework. The single parent doesn't know what to do at this point.

Remember, single parent, God gave you the responsibility to handle your own children. But because of circumstances that may have occurred, you have to get a job to make ends meet. You have other people watching your children, but you don't know for sure if one of them is being abused. In desperation, you close your eyes. You drop your children off to stay with strangers. You may not come home until midnight, and your son is home with a stranger who doesn't care about him. Yes, you're out there making ends meet, but you have an 8-year-old boy whose future is at stake. Whatever he's going to become in the future, it's at stake now. If he's going to become a lawyer, a doctor, a policeman, whatever, the foundation for accomplishment has to start now.

If you leave him home alone, no one will be there to give him clear direction. No one will be there to tell him when it's play time, homework time, bath time, or time to say his prayers and go to bed. Mommy is not home to tell him anything, and he doesn't listen to the caregiver you left him with. And some of the sitters don't care because he's not their child. Then by the time you come in, he's asleep and you have had no interaction with your child all day. There is no relationship between you. From 7:00 A.M. in the morning until midnight, your child had no fellowship with you. It doesn't matter how many kisses you put on his cheek, they won't replace interaction.

It's possible that when your child was just eight years old, he sometimes skipped school. Because you worked 12-15 hours a day, he figured you wouldn't know the difference. So, even at that young age, he hung out and did what he wanted. This young boy who had an entire world of dreams before him has had his life shattered because no one was there to protect him. Even animals protect their children better than human beings. They go out of their way to ensure that no one comes in and hurts their young. If you see a lion, you dare not touch her cub—you'll get your hands bitten off.

When eagles leave their nest, you'll see them hovering nearby. You dare not touch their nest. By the time your fingers touch it, they'd be down to get you. All animals shield their young from harm.

You may work two jobs in order to give the kids all the brand name clothes and designer shoes they want and all the toys they beg you for, but you're not protecting them. Where is all of the money you've invested in your children going? It's probably not going into something of lasting value like a college fund or savings bonds.

Soon the justice system has to deal with your children because you didn't discipline them *yourself*. You weren't firm and said you couldn't afford the latest computer game. You took a second job in order to buy them all the toys they wanted. You should say, "As long as my rent, light bill, and certain basic necessities are paid, one job is enough.

These are definitely big pressures that you need to deal with, but handle them God's way. Consider quitting the second job and taking over once again in your household. Find out what's going on with your children. Become active in their lives both physically and emotionally. They are the biggest responsibility you will ever have.

Take stock of where your kids are and don't leap into marriage just to alleviate a problem. Let God lead you into a marriage so that He can bless it and help you with all of the adjustments that your family will need to make along the way.

*Insufficiency
makes singles think
they don't have enough
money to get married.
They feel pressure from
society to be extravagant.
If you can't afford one thing,
do something else so that
you can stay within
your budget.*

CHAPTER TWELVE
Insufficiency

Finally, the fifth pressure singles face is *insufficiency*. Time is all-important in today's fast paced world. We never seem to have enough time for the important things. Singles are so busy working to buy nice furniture so they can get married, they don't have time to do things together. We drive nice cars, but we don't have enough time to spend with one another because we're working. God wants you to have the best, but there is a problem here. We're stressing ourselves out to achieve a lot of material things so we can "start our marriage off right," but we're sacrificing the success of the relationship by not taking the time to really get to know each other better.

Insufficiency makes singles think they don't have enough money to get married. They feel pressure from society to be extravagant. If you can't afford one thing, do something else so that you can stay within your budget. (It will be good practice for after your marriage.) Why go out and struggle for years to earn enough money to pay for the caterer, the food, and the decorations just to impress others with a fancy wedding? Get your family together and have a simple ceremony that you can afford.

Many rich people don't have big weddings. Celebrities often go off to a private place so their wedding can be secluded. When most rich people get married, they have a little tent erected on the back of their estate and have a private ceremony there. A little truck backs up into the yard and a caterer serves the food. Many who don't have the funds want the whole world to come to their wedding. If you have $5000, maybe you should spend $1000 on the wedding and the rest can be used for the honeymoon, although it's best to keep some in savings. Stop trying to impress people. Have a wedding that fits your budget.

Let's say you've saved for two years to get married. What if the moment you get back from your honeymoon both of you are laid off from work? You

Insufficiency

probably don't have a month's rent saved. You won't know what to do the next day. You don't even have $100 in your savings account. I don't want you to make the same mistake that others consistently make. You don't have to live from paycheck to paycheck because you're trying to please people. Live within your means. It will bring much peace to your life.

Dealing with these five difficulties—social pressures, isolation, sexual pleasure, parenting, and insufficiency—in a relationship will help you resolve conflicts quicker and create a stable environment in which you can deepen your relationship.

Beyond Passion

Let God give you a vision for your life. Ask Him to infuse you with purpose in everything you do. And read His Word to develop a passion in you to see it all come to pass. When you do these things, it will make dating God's way the best thing that ever happened to you!

CHAPTER THIRTEEN

Under Construction

Except the Lord build the house, they labour in vain that build it; except the Lord keep the city, the watchman waketh but in vain. (Psalm 127:1)

You're a person who is now under construction. God is preparing you according to His plan. In the construction of a building, you start with a blueprint. A blueprint tells everyone what the building will eventually look like. God placed within each of you the blueprint or vision of what He wants you to become.

The Blueprint

Imagine beginning the construction of a building and assembling the carpenters, the bricklayers, and the electrical engineers all together. What if there were no blueprint for these people to follow? The electrician might say, "Well, I'm just going to hang those lights wherever I want to. If I want to hang them on the floor, I'll do that." Can you imagine the chaos if every tradesman worked that way on this building? Without a blueprint, nothing of substance would get accomplished. A person without a vision, a plan, a purpose, an insight of where he wants to go, will live in chaos and get nowhere in life.

But just having a blueprint is not enough. You have to follow the details of it. You're not going to get anywhere in life if you don't follow the plan. If you don't say to yourself, "God, show me my purpose on earth. God, I'm not going to just work day in and day out and pay rent somewhere. I'm not going to just take a woman, have sex with her, give her children, then eat and go to sleep. I know there's more to life than that."

What is your vision for your life? If you should die today, would people say they will truly miss a talented person, a gifted person, a person who lived up to his potential, or would they say you served no purpose?

Do you have a blueprint? Do you purpose in your heart that you're going to go somewhere in life? Do you say, "God it's my desire to establish myself and therefore move my future family into a better community than where I live now. I have a vision to gradually climb the ladder of success to the next level. This is my desire, this is my dream. This is where I want to go in life."

Getting the Vision

How do you begin construction? You must have a heart to find your vision. Singles desperately need to know where they're going so they can begin to travel down the right road. Start thinking about what you want to become in life.

Every day I live and breathe my vision. I have my vision documented in a folder. These papers spell out just what I want to accomplish over a period of so many years. It may not happen in the time frame I've set, but at least I have a vision and plan and have begun working on it. You may decide to complete a house by a certain time, and it just doesn't work. There are always setbacks: bad weather, late delivery of materials, etc. There are circumstances that will result in not having your house done by the time you had planned. But you have begun the house, and you will eventually complete it because you have held onto the vision.

Do you want to see yourself eventually move out of the area in which you live? Do you have a desire to move into a better community? Do you have a vision to be debt free? Do you have a vision to raise a strong family? Do you have a vision to be financially independent? What are your goals? What is your purpose? What do you envision five years from now?

Purpose

The second thing you need in construction is a purpose. What purpose will the various rooms of your house have? You must know before you can construct them. So too, you must have purpose in your life. If you have a vision, then your purpose will be to accomplish the vision that God has given you.

Singles with vision and purpose will let nothing stand in their way; they are filled with faith. Those who believe in themselves are people of faith. Even if others speak negative things about you, you have to believe that you will fulfill your purpose and vision. Look at Job. His wife didn't encourage him to walk through the suffering and the affliction. She hadn't consulted God's purpose for their lives when she said "Are you still holding on to your integrity? Curse God and die!" (Job 2:9) But Job believed in himself. He believed in God and he said, "Though he slay me, I am going to trust him" (Job 13:15).

Reasons to Marry Someone

Women, some of you do not believe in yourselves. Some of you feel inadequate if you don't have a husband walking beside you. You think everyone will see that your building is only half complete if you don't get married soon. You see other women with their husbands, and you ask God when you're going to get yours. You don't want a man for God's purposes, you only want a man for social recognition and identification purposes. You want someone to look at you and say, "Yeah, she's achieved something. She's not walking by herself." Don't let the devil put foolish ideas in your head and tell you that you are incomplete without a man. Don't say to yourself, *I have to get a husband. I'm a nobody without one.*

Here's what you can do. Ask yourself these questions before you get into a relationship with a man. *What is he bringing to the table that I don't already have?* Do I need a car? No, I have one. Do I need somewhere to live? No. Do I need a job? No. What is he bringing to the table? If he's not bringing anything to the relationship, you're not thinking clearly. Don't let yourself be used by him.

Men, if the women shape up, you won't be able to wreck their lives the way you do now. How? When you make a lot of promises to them that you don't fulfill, but they give in to your sexual demands anyway. When some women meet a man that they think they love, and he says he loves them and promises them the entire world, they give in. Instead, women, keep your body holy and say, "Until you bring something to the table, do not touch this." If the woman says "No," you have to bring some things she doesn't have to the table—the ring, the license, the bank account, and especially a commitment and a vision. She needs to know where you're going to take her in life.

Passion

Besides having vision and purpose, you must have a passion. At the age of 36, I made up my mind that I was not going to be the average black man. I refuse to let society say that because I'm a black man I'm unable to succeed. I told myself I will be successful.

I found out what God called me to do. Obviously everyone knows He called me to be a pastor, but I know that I have many other gifts in me. Several years ago, I wrote my first book and had no idea that it would be so successful. It turned out that thousands of copies were sold. Now I'm working on four more books to be published this year and next that will be a blessing to the body of Christ.

My life is organized in such a way that if I chose to quit preaching I could do so, and it wouldn't hurt me financially. All of my finances don't come from my church position alone. I didn't put all of my eggs into one basket. If you were to go to work Monday and found out that you were laid off, do you have any other income that could sustain you? If your answer is "no," you could be in deep trouble some day.

You must begin to dream. Men, your fiancé may be wondering whether you're going to take the leadership role. It isn't that you *can't* do it, it's that you must have a *passion* to do it. You don't need a lot of money to begin with. You just have to have a passion to succeed no matter what.

In 1996 my wife and I said we wanted to get out of the community where we lived because the property value was going down. We hesitated for about two years. I had no money, but I had a vision. I decided I was going to take the lead and somehow work it out so that we could move. I didn't sit there and dream. No. I told myself I can do all things through Christ who strengthens me. I spoke life into my situation.

We saw a community under construction that we loved. No buildings were there at the time, and there were no trees or landscaping either except for the man-made lakes. All you saw were piles of sand, dirt, and rocks all over the place. This was empty undeveloped land, but the builders had the blueprint. They knew it was going to become something special. We said, "Let's do it now even though we have no money." We didn't know where the money would come from, but we said we have to move. My wife and I held hands as we stood alone on the property. We prayed, "God, You've done it before for us, and we know You'll do it again. We are believing you, God. We want You to help us build this house. We're going to do it and believe that it's not going to be a struggle."

I didn't have the money, but I had a vision and believed that God wanted us to live there. I saw with a passion where I could secure the future of my family. Shortly after our prayer, the Lord graciously provided the money for us to purchase the house. Nine months later, our home stood on the land that had once been undeveloped. In the beginning, I hadn't seen how it could be financially possible, but I had a vision, a purpose, and a passion to see it come to pass.

Singles, ask God to give you the same passion for yourself and your future partner. Let God give you a vision for your life. Ask Him to infuse you with purpose in everything you do. And read His Word to develop a passion in you to see it all come to pass. When you do these things, it will make dating God's way the best thing that ever happened to you!

For more information about Bishop Fernandez or to book speaking engagements, write to:

Henry Fernandez Ministries
P.O. Box 9726
Ft. Lauderdale, FL 33310

Also by Henry Fernandez

Divine Love
Henry Fernandez shares practical ways to express the divine love that God has placed in our hearts. It's the kind of love that counts when human love isn't enough. *Divine Love* is a great book for individuals, couples, and for family or small group Bible studies.
ISBN 1-58169-006-1   64 pg. PB $6.95

Faith: The Key to Success
A breakthrough book that will show you how to move the "mountains' that stand between you and your success (it's not what you think). You'll also learn how to go through testings and trials—all the while rejoicing at what God is doing in you through them.
ISBN 1-58169-065-7   192 pg. hardcover $18.99

Available from your local bookstore, Amazon.com, BN.com or call 888-670-7463